I0410394

# My Favorite Dino's Coloring Book
### By Joe L. Blevins

ISBN-13: 978-1539916437

ISBN-10: 153991643X

To Arrow, Tabitha, and Sarah.
Also: to Mister Jakub, who also loves
Dinosaurs. Me too!

Some Tyrannosaurs Rex, while out hunting. Cretaceous period. Meat eaters. Therapod family of dinosaurs.

Some Tyrannosaurs Rex on patrol. Cretaceous period. Meat eaters.

A Stegosaurus family on an afternoon walk. Cretaceous period. Plant eaters.

A Stegosaurus play date. Fun in the sun.

Apatosaurus in love. Cretaceous period.

Apatosaurus-plant eaters. Early Cretaceous period. They breathed out of the top of their heads, where the bony crest appears.

Triceratops and Hadrosaurs/"Duckbills" love their veggies!

A few T-rexes encounter some Pachycephalosarus. (Their heads had a 'boney helmet' built in.) They butted heads with enemies. They were plant eaters. No one likes bullies, especially some tough Pachycephalosarus.

Spinosaurus. Meat eater, Land lover and avid swimmer. Weighs about 10 tons. Meaner than a T-Rex. Cretaceous period.

A T-Rex cousin that lived in the artic areas. Late Jurassic period. 20 tons by weight.

Hadrosaurs moving to a new place. ("Duck-billed" dinosaurs.) Also called "Maiasaura" dinosaurs. ("Good mother") Plant eaters. Much like a modern cow.

Two T-Rex's on patrol. Looking for some trouble.

Playing "hide and seek."

"Tag...you're 'IT'!"
(Brontosaurus kisses the top of the T-Rex's head.)

Hylaeosarus (Clubbed Tail's) and Ornitholestes (small T-Rex relatives/pack hunters) Therapod family of dinosaurs.

A Delaposaurus or "Spitter." Meat eater. Creataceous period.

Pterodactyl nest, with hatching dino's.

Oliraptorosaurs are early birds, and warm-blooded, ancestors. They are dinosaurs that had feathers and could leap and fly a short distance. The weighed about twenty pounds. And two feet tall at maturity. They had teeth and a flock mentality with many banding together for protection against predators.

An Oliraptorosaurs mother tries to protect her young from danger. A feathered dinosaur and an early bird.

Mosasaur detail. At the Ammonite luncheon.

A hungry Plegasaur dinosaur and a large Ammonite: (Texanite) Nautilus family.

Tylasaur/Mosasaur family. Ammonites: Rare Texanite and straight Bacculites/Nautilus family. Jellyfish, sea snakes and small Piper fish,

At low tide the water dinosaurs went along the beach to eat something tasty for dinner. A mosasaur/Tylasaurus family. Cretaceous period. 75 million years ago.

A comet arrives.

# The End

**Books by Joe Blevins LLC. © 2016-11-04**

**Books by Joe Blevins LLC.**

Search www.amazon.com

Find : BOOKS

Then see : joe blevins

www.hattrick2014.jb@gmail.com

**www.blevinsbooks.wordpress.com**

# Read to a friend.
# Be a friend!

Joe L. Blevins is an author of over fifteen years and an illustrator for over forty years. Blevins' books range from horror, historical, and more family oriented tales. Joe's stories always use an element of history as a base for the premise. Joe uses life events and details to let his stories ring true to the reader. Most of all: reading is to be fun and informative for all ages. Joe worked for twenty-six years in electronics, and twelve years as a teacher at three different school districts. While he acted as a teacher he was involved in various reading programs. There he saw a need to make better stories for young readers. He saw what the students liked and what they did not. This was his real "education" as an author by learning that readers demand more than just a good story. They need something that "speaks" to them as a person. These are books that the reader can actually relate to. Blevins worked with many students with learning disabilities. He also worked with some hearing impaired students. These students needed a story tailored for their needs with brightly colored illustrations to keep the reader interested. Joe continues to write with his series, Deux fois les ennuis; Cowboy Colton, and Gaston's Nursery Rhymes.  Now some coloring books with "Pixie Land" and many others you might enjoy. Blevins writes for children and those that love to read to them. Now M. Joe Blevins has teamed up with Madame Louise Lamontague for these new books in some exciting French language versions. Joe invites you to read his stories and make comments, if you wish. Thank you.

# My Favorite Dino's Coloring Book

## By Joe L. Blevins

ISBN-13: 978-1539916437

ISBN-10: 153991643X

www.ingramcontent.com/pod-product-compliance
Lightning Source LLC
Chambersburg PA
CBHW081750280526
45789CB00008B/2804